Nature's Cycles

The Water Cycle

Sally Morgan

PowerKiDS press

New York

Published in 2009 by The Rosen Publishing Group Inc.
29 East 21st Street, New York, NY 10010

First Edition

Series editor: Nicola Edwards
Designer: Jason Billin

Library of Congress Cataloging-in-Publication Data

Morgan, Sally.
  The water cycle / Sally Morgan. — 1st ed.
      p. cm. — (Nature's cycles)
  Includes index.
  ISBN 978-1-4358-2868-1 (library binding)
  ISBN 978-1-4358-2950-3 (paperback)
  ISBN 978-1-4358-2954-1 (6-pack)
  1. Hydrologic cycle—Juvenile literature. I. Title.
  GB848.M66 2009
  551.48—dc22
                              2008025810

Manufactured in China

Picture acknowledgments: Cover: Main image: Reinhardt Dirscherl/ Ecoscene;
river Wayne Lawler/ Ecoscene; cloud Sally Morgan/ Ecoscene; glacier Graham
Neden/Ecoscene

Title page: Reinhardt Dirscherl/ Ecoscene; p2 Wayne Lawler/ Ecoscene; p3
Robert Pickett / Ecoscene – Papilio; p4 Neeraj Mishra/ Ecoscene; p5 Fritz
Polking/ Ecoscene; p6 Graham Neden/ Ecoscene; p7 (t) Paul Thompson/
Ecoscene, (b) Robert Pickett / Ecoscene – Papilio; p8 NASA; p9 Wayne
Lawler/ Ecoscene; p10 Peter Hulme/ Ecoscene; p11 Photographer's name tbc
Ecoscene; p12 (t) Paul Thompson/ Ecoscene, (ml) NASA, (mr) Robert Walker/
Ecoscene; p13 (t) Sally Morgan/ Ecoscene, (m) Robert Walker/ Ecoscene,
(b) Paul Thompson/ Ecoscene; p14 Fritz Polking/ Ecoscene; p15 Mike
Whittle/ Ecoscene; p16 Wayne Lawler/ Ecoscene; p17 Wayne Lawler/
Ecoscene; p18 Andria Massey/ Ecoscene; p19 Alan Towse/ Ecoscene;
p20 Kieran Murray/ Ecoscene; p21 Alexandra Jones/ Ecoscene;
p22 Alan Towse/ Ecoscene; p23 Tony Page/ Ecoscene; p24 (t, m)
Vicki Coombs/ Ecoscene, (b) Alan Towse/ Ecoscene; p25 Chinch
Gryniewicz/ Ecoscene; p26 Mick Blowfield/ Ecoscene; p27 NASA;
p28 Angela Hampton/ Ecoscene; p29 (t, b) Wayne Lawler/ Ecoscene

Contents

Water for life

Water is essential for life on Earth. Without it, life could not exist. Earth is often called the blue planet, because more than two-thirds of its surface is covered by oceans.

▼ Animals, such as these monkeys, need clean water.

Every living organism contains water. Water makes up about three-quarters of our bodies. That's about 9.25 gallons (35 liters) in a teenager. Some organisms contain even more water, for example, jellyfish can be more than 95 percent water. Water is an important habitat, too, for animals such as fish, seals, and whales, and plants such as seaweeds. Animals and plants that live in water are called aquatic.

In Focus: Plants and water

Plants need water. They obtain their water from the soil through their roots. Water is carried through their stems to the leaves. Then water evaporates from the leaves. If plants do not get enough water from the soil, their leaves will droop. This is called wilting. Without water, the leaves will shrivel and the plant may die.

The world's water

Most of the world's water is salt water. This is water that contains salt and which cannot be drunk. The water that occurs in rivers, lakes, and glaciers is fresh water. Fresh water makes up less than 3 percent of all the Earth's water. Fresh water is virtually all water with just a few natural minerals. This is the water that comes out of faucets and that people need for drinking and washing.

The amount of water on the Earth is constant, so it is continuously recycled between the atmosphere, rivers, and seas. This forms the water cycle or hydrological cycle. The cycle starts with water falling as rain and snow onto the ground. The water seeps into the soil and into streams and rivers. Then water evaporates from all surfaces back into the atmosphere.

● Fresh water pours over this waterfall. Waterfalls occur on rivers where there is a sudden change in height of the riverbed. Here, fresh water cascades over rocks to reach the lower part of the river.

Investigate: How much of an apple is water?

See if you can find out how much water an apple contains. Take a fresh apple and weigh it. Record its mass. Now cut the apple into slices and place the slices on a plate on a sunny windowsill, so that they dry out. When the slices are dry and leathery, weigh them again. How much does the apple weigh now? How much mass has the apple lost? The difference in mass is due to the loss of water.

Why is water special?

Water is the most common liquid on Earth. It is odorless and colorless. Water is made up of one type of molecule that is formed from one atom of oxygen and two atoms of hydrogen. Its chemical formula is written as H_2O.

Changing state

Water can exist in solid form as ice, as a liquid, and as a gas called water vapor. Earth is the only planet in the solar system that has the right conditions for water to exist in all three states. At 32°F (0°C), water changes from solid to liquid and at 212°F (100°C), it boils and becomes a vapor.

Ice is made from lots of water molecules that are bonded or joined closely together so they cannot move. When water freezes, it expands and it becomes less dense. This means that ice floats on the top of liquid water. This is why a layer of ice forms over ponds and lakes during cold weather. Icebergs are formed from solid ice and they float on the oceans.

⬤ All three states of water can be seen in this photograph. There is water vapor in the air, liquid water in the sea, and frozen water in the glacier.

Investigate: Water's color

If you hold up a clear container of water, you see that water is transparent. It has no color. But when you look at the sea on a sunny day, it looks blue. This is because of the way light reflects off of the surface of the water. Part of the color is a reflection of the blue sky. But some of the color comes from tiny particles floating in the water. They absorb red light and reflect blue light.

Water temperature

Amazingly, the temperature of the water that makes up the oceans does not alter much. This is because water can absorb a lot of the sun's heat energy without becoming much warmer. That is why the sea can still feel very cool in the middle of summer. However, the seas can hold on to heat and do not cool down quickly, either. So in the winter, the water can feel quite warm compared to the land. This creates a very stable environment for marine organisms.

⬤ Water in a glass looks clear.

⬤ Surface tension prevents the water strider from sinking into the water.

In Focus: Surface tension

A water strider can walk on water. This is possible because of the property of water called surface tension. The molecules of water at the surface grip each other tightly and form a kind of skin. This is strong enough to support the weight of an insect such as a water strider, enabling it to skim over the surface.

Fresh and salt water

Thousands of millions of years ago, there were no oceans on Earth. The Earth was so hot that any water quickly boiled away. The atmosphere was full of steam pumped out by the many volcanoes. Then, as the Earth cooled down over many millions of years, the steam turned to water and rain fell. The water level rose and mountains disappeared under water. Large depressions on the Earth's surface filled with water and became oceans. The water was salty, because the steam from the volcanoes was rich in salts.

Deep oceans

There are five oceans in the world; Atlantic, Pacific, Indian, Arctic, and Southern. The depth of the oceans varies, but it is an average of about 2.2 miles (3.5 kilometers). Beneath the waves are mountain ranges, active volcanoes, and long, seemingly bottomless trenches. The deepest ocean trench is the Mariana Trench in the Pacific. At its deepest point, it is around 7 mi. (11 km) deep and it could easily swallow the Himalayas.

◀ Two-thirds of the Earth's surface is covered by the oceans.

Within the oceans, the water is moving. Warm water is less dense than cold water, so it rises above the cold water. In the oceans, there is a layer of warm water that lies over cold water. There are currents of water moving through the oceans, too. For example, there is a flow of warm water called the Gulf Stream that forms off the coast of North America and travels across the Atlantic to Northern Europe. There are cold currents, too, such as the current that flows from the Antarctic up the west coast of Africa.

Fresh water

Most of the Earth's fresh water is locked up as ice in the polar ice caps and in glaciers. Some forms rivers and lakes and the rest is found in the ground. When rain falls, it runs off into streams and rivers. Some water seeps into the ground. This is groundwater, and it drains down through the rock until it reaches a layer of rock that it cannot pass. The water collects in the rock above this impermeable layer.

⊙ Water pours out of a well that has been dug down to an aquifer.

In Focus: Aquifers

An underground layer of water-filled rock is called an aquifer. An aquifer is an important store of water. Water may remain trapped in an aquifer for a long time. In Egypt, there are aquifers where it is estimated that up to 40,000 years may have passed between the time water fell to the ground and the time it reaches the surface again.

Evaporation and condensation

Evaporation and condensation are two key processes in the water cycle. Evaporation is the change in state of water from a liquid to a vapor. Condensation is the change from a vapor to a liquid.

Evaporation

Evaporation is caused by liquid water being heated and given heat energy. The heat causes the molecules in the liquid water to move around more quickly and bump into each other. Some molecules have enough energy to break away from the other molecules and turn into water vapor. This is called evaporation.

Water can evaporate at almost any temperature above freezing point. For example, after rain there are puddles on the ground. When the sun shines, the water evaporates into a vapor and the puddle disappears. Water also evaporates when it is boiled in a pot or kettle. The steam emerging from the surface or spout contains a lot of water vapor.

◀ A geyser is a spout of hot water and steam that escapes from a crack in the ground under very high pressure.

◗ Seawater contains about three percent salt. Salt is obtained from seawater by trapping the water in shallow salt pans. When water evaporates, the salt is left behind.

In Focus: Antifreeze

Water usually freezes at 32°F (0°C). However, if there are other substances in the water, such as salts, the freezing point is lower.

Water circulates in a car's radiator to stop the engine from overheating. When temperatures fall below freezing, there is a chance that the water could freeze. Water expands when it freezes and this could crack the pipes. To prevent this, people add antifreeze to the radiator water to lower its freezing point and make it less likely to freeze.

Some animals can make a kind of antifreeze, too. For example, the ice fish that lives under the ice of the Antarctic creates a substance that stops its cells freezing.

Condensation

Water vapor rises into the atmosphere. As it rises, it cools. This causes it to condense, or change state back into a liquid. The water droplets fall back to the ground as rain.

Often condensation can be seen on windows. In the winter, for example, the air outside a house is colder than the air inside. When water vapor inside comes into contact with the cold window glass, it condenses and droplets of water form on the inside of the window.

Investigate: Make your own water cycle

Create a mini-water cycle on a windowsill. Take a small pot plant, water it, and place it in a large plastic bag. Tie the bag so that the air cannot escape. Place the bag with the plant inside on a sunny windowsill. The heat causes water to evaporate from the leaves and soil. The water vapor condenses on the inside of the bag and runs down the sides to collect at the bottom.

Clouds and the water cycle

When water vapor rises in the atmosphere, it cools and condenses. This forms clouds. The clouds are made up of droplets of water, which get bigger and bigger. Eventually, these droplets become so heavy that they fall as rain. Clouds vary in their shape and appearance. The three main types of cloud are cumulus, stratus, and cirrus.

Water vapor cools and condenses, forming clouds.

The Water Cycle

Water evaporates from all surfaces.

Rivers and oceans fill with rainwater.

Water droplets fall from clouds as rain.

Cumulus clouds

Cumulus clouds are puffy and they look a little like pulled-apart cotton balls. They tend to form when warm moist air is pushed upward. As the air cools, the water condenses and a cumulus cloud forms. Summer thunderstorms are usually caused by cumulonimbus clouds. These are large dark clouds that are not very puffy. They tower high in the sky and bring heavy rain, thunder, and lightning.

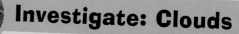

Investigate: Clouds

Using the photographs on this page and on the Internet, see if you can identify the different types of cloud that move across the sky. Can you link the clouds to the varying forms of weather?

Stratus clouds

The word stratus comes from the Latin meaning "spread out." Stratus clouds are horizontal, flat clouds that spread out across the sky like a blanket. These clouds usually form where a layer of warm, moist air passes over a layer of cooler air. When the warm air comes into contact with the cool air, water vapor condenses to form cloud. These clouds are associated with rain.

Cirrus clouds

Cirrus clouds are thin, featherlike clouds that form about 3–4 miles (5–7 km) high in the sky. At that height, it is so cold that the water condenses to form ice crystals. Cirrus clouds are seen on fine, sunny days.

In Focus: Elephants and thunderstorms

Water is very important to elephants since they drink many quarts each day and use it to clean their skin. However, African elephants live in areas where there are dry seasons with no rain, followed by rainy seasons. The start of the rainy season is marked by frequent thunderstorms. Researchers have discovered that the elephants can sense a thunderstorm more than 62 miles (100 km) away. They can detect vibrations in the ground caused by the thunder. As soon as they hear the thunderstorm, they start walking toward it, because they know that it brings water.

Water and weather

The water cycle has an important role to play in our daily weather. It is responsible for rain, snow, sleet, and hail.

Weather or climate?

Our daily weather is made up of a combination of wind, water, and heat from the sun. The mix of different amounts of sunshine, cloud, and rainfall varies from one day to the next. Climate is the usual pattern of weather that a particular place experiences. For example, areas near the equator have a tropical climate that is warm and sunny all year round.

⬢ Blizzards are common in the Antarctic. The strong winds blow the snow around, making it difficult for the Emperor Penguins to find their way around.

Investigate: Rainfall

The annual rainfall in the Amazon region of South America is a massive 394 in. (1,000 cm). In contrast, some of the driest deserts in the world receive less than 1 inch (2.5 cm) a year. See if you can find out the rainfall of the area in which you live. Can you research whether the rainfall has changed much over the last 100 years? Many public libraries have information on local history.

Extreme weather

Our everyday lives depend on there being enough water. In some parts of the world, droughts are common, and there is no rain for months, or even years. This lack of water causes plants and animals to die. Crop failures can cause food shortages or even famine. In contrast, if there is too much rain, flooding may occur. A storm can bring heavy rainfall in a short period of time. Soon, rivers swell and burst their banks and there is widespread flooding.

▶ Life goes on as usual in this Vietnamese town, despite the heavy monsoon rain.

Monsoon rain

In some parts of the world, there are periods of heavy rain called monsoons. The people have to cope with heavy rain falling almost daily for several months. Then there is little rain for the rest of the year. India has a monsoon climate. In the summer, winds blow off the Indian Ocean and they bring rain. Heavy monsoon rain falls from June to September. At times, the rain is torrential, causing widespread flooding and land slides. In the winter, dry winds blow from the northeast, and the weather is hot and arid.

In Focus: Stopping floods

Millions of people live near rivers and their homes can be at risk from flooding. Floods can be prevented by building barriers along river banks to stop water from flowing over low-lying land. Some towns are protected by flood barriers that close at times of flood risk. Sometimes the flood water can be directed to farmland beside the river, so that homes are not damaged.

Rivers

Much of the water that falls to the ground drains into a river. The rivers run across the land and empty into the sea.

River stages

When rain falls on hilly ground, some of its soaks into the ground, but the rest runs downhill. First, it forms a stream that tumbles down the slope. As more water enters the stream, it becomes a river. Fast-flowing river water is powerful and has lots of energy. It wears away the banks and the bed of the river. Small rocks are picked up and carried downstream. The rocks rub against each other and are worn down. As they become smaller, they form sediment, which is made up of many tiny particles of sand, silt, and mud.

Once the river reaches the less hilly ground, the water flows more slowly. It may form bends, or meanders. By the time the river eventually reaches the sea, it has dropped all its sediment.

▼ The water flows slowly along this meandering river.

Animals that live in fast-moving water are specially adapted to this difficult environment. For example, freshwater mussels have sticky threads to attach themselves to rocks, and leeches have suckers to hang on to plants. Water plants have adaptations, too, such as well-developed roots so they do not get washed away.

⬇ This delta, with its network of islands and channels, has formed at the mouth of a river in Australia.

Estuaries and deltas

Estuaries and deltas form where rivers enter the sea. An estuary forms where the currents are strong enough to move the sediment out to sea, keeping the mouth of the river open, for example, the Thames Estuary in the United Kingdom. Deltas form where the sediment is not removed. Instead, it builds up into marshy islands, for example, the Mississippi Delta in the United States and the Nile Delta in Egypt. The river splits up into many small channels that wind their way around the islands to the sea. Over time, the delta grows larger, until it extends into the sea.

Investigate: Sedimentation

A fast-flowing river has lots of energy and it can carry many particles. As the river starts to slow down, the water loses energy and the particles are dropped. The heaviest particles are dropped first, and the lightest last. You can see how the different sizes of particles settle in this simple investigation. Collect a mixture of sand, gravel, and soil and pour it into a see-through plastic bottle. Add enough water to cover. Replace the cap and shake the bottle vigorously. Leave the bottle on the side for a week, to allow all the particles to settle. Which particles settled first at the bottom of the bottle?

Water for drinking

People need water for many different uses, such as drinking, cooking, washing, and cleaning. This water is taken from streams and rivers, lakes, and wells. If too much is taken, it can disrupt the water cycle.

○ Collecting water from a well on the street is a daily chore for women in many less developed countries.

Water use

People who live in more developed countries, such as Australia, the United States, and the United Kingdom, use much more water than people living in less developed countries, such as Tanzania and Pakistan. The highest use of water occurs in the U.S., where each person uses about 160 gallons (600 liters) of water a day. Each person in the U.K. uses about 40 gallons (150 liters) a day. In less developed countries, the figure is as low as 5 gallons (20 liters) a day. Also, many people in less developed countries do not have water piped into their home. They have to collect their water from a standpipe in the street or a local well. Around the world, millions of women spend several hours each day just fetching water. Often, the water is not safe to drink and it has to be boiled first.

Gallons of water are used each day in this town in Florida to keep the roadside verges green.

Investigate: Daily water usage

How much water do you use each day? Make a diary that records how much you use. If you have a water meter, you can take a reading and see how much water is used in a week. Can you work out how much you and your family use each year? Can you think of ways of cutting back on your water use?

Disrupting the water cycle

The water cycle can be easily disrupted and this can have widespread consequences. If too much water is taken from a well, the water seeping down from the surface may not be able to replace the water being pumped out of the ground. Gradually, the water level in the ground falls. The well runs dry and a new, deeper well has to be dug.

In Focus: Water and disease

Safe drinking water is essential for health. Water can carry disease-causing organisms, such as bacteria, viruses, and parasites. If drinking water is not treated properly, the disease-causing organisms can enter the body and cause disease. A staggering 1.8 million people die each year from diarrhea. Many of these people are children under the age of five. Up to half of all people living in less developed countries suffer from a health problem caused by poor quality drinking water and inadequate sewage treatment.

Polluted water

For hundreds of years, people have used rivers and the sea as a place to dump their waste. Untreated sewage from bathrooms was emptied into rivers along with chemical waste and garbage. In London in the 1900s, for example, there was so much sewage in the crowded city that the stench hanging over the area at night was almost intolerable.

A lot of chemicals are used in farming. When pests attack their crops, farmers may spray a pesticide to kill them, or use a weed killer to keep weeds under control. Water carries these chemicals from the fields into streams, rivers, and the sea, where they harm aquatic life.

Oil spills

Oil can pollute water. Oil may leak from storage tanks into rivers, and accidents may cause oil tankers to spill thousands of gallons of oil into the sea. The oil spreads over the surface of the water, creating a slick. It clogs the feathers of birds and smothers small animals. Cleaning up the oil is a dirty job. Often, the oil is simply skimmed off the surface and washed off of rocks. Detergents can be used to break up the oil, but the detergents can harm aquatic animals, too.

◯ This oil tanker ran aground off the coast of Shetland, U.K., in 1993, causing an oil slick that spread along many miles of previously unspoilt coastline.

You can use the Internet to find out if your local river or beach is clean. Look up organizations that are responsible for water quality. Do you have a favorite beach? In Europe, the Blue Flag scheme identifies beaches that have safe swimming water.

Too many nutrients

Fertilizers and sewage are full of nutrients. If they enter a river, the nutrients cause microorganisms, such as bacteria, to increase in number. These microorganisms use up a lot of the oxygen in the water. This leaves little oxygen for other aquatic organisms, such as fish, and they die.

Sometimes, as a result of too many nutrients in the water, rivers become covered in a thick layer of fast-growing green algae. The algae spread across the surface of the river, blocking the light to the aquatic plants below and causing them to die.

As rivers become more polluted, aquatic animals disappear. First to go are the larger fish, such as salmon and trout, followed by small insects and other invertebrates.

These fish have been killed by a lack of oxygen in the water.

In Focus: Cleaning rivers

Many countries now have strict laws that control the quality of water in rivers. There are laws controlling what substances can be put into the river, and how often. The quality of the water is tested regularly, and industries have to make sure that their waste water does not contain harmful chemicals, otherwise they are fined. As river water has become cleaner, fish such as salmon have returned.

Down the drain

Do you know what happens to the water that disappears down the drain or toilet? In many homes, waste water from kitchens and bathrooms empties into the drains and is carried along pipes to a sewage works, where it is treated. This waste water contains sewage (waste from the toilet) together with soapy water.

In the past, sewage and waste water was emptied straight into a river or sea without any treatment. Now, many countries have laws that state that sewage has to be treated before it can be emptied into a river or the sea.

The final stage of treatment for waste water in this area of Florida takes place in a marsh, where the plants complete the cleaning process.

A cruise ship is a little like a small floating town. The people on board produce a great deal of waste water. An average cruise ship produces 1,320 gallons (5,000 liters) of sewage and 7,925 gallons (30,000 liters) of gray water a day! Until recently, this was dumped untreated into the sea. In 2005, new rules were agreed that all cruise ships would be fitted with a sewage treatment plant by 2010. However, raw sewage can be still be dumped in the sea so long as the cruise ship is 12 miles (19 kilometers) from land.

⬤ These huge cruise liners carry several thousand people, who all produce waste.

Recycling "gray" water

In some homes, waste water from baths and washing machines is recycled. This water is called "gray water," because it contains soap. It can be used for flushing toilets. Some people pipe the water from their baths into yards to water plants in the summer. This helps reduce the amount of water used.

Industrial waste water

Some manufacturing processes generate a lot of waste water, for example, every ton of paper produces 10,570 gallons (40,000 liters) of waste water, and for every gallon of gasoline there are 18 gallons of dirty water. Waste water from industry has to be treated before it can enter a river or the sea. Many factories and industrial plants have their own water treatment plant.

Farmers have waste water, too, such as slurry, the waste washed out of barns where animals are housed. This has to be stored in huge slurry tanks, so it does not drain straight into rivers.

Investigate: Waste disposal

Some waste, such as cooking oil, bleach, and paint, should never be poured down the drain. It's not safe to pour away pesticides, such as plant sprays, either. All these liquids have to be stored in their containers and taken to a special disposal site. Often people store unwanted chemicals in a garage or basement. What does your family do with unwanted paint? Use the Internet to find out where to dispose of old paint cans.

Cleaning water

Most towns and cities around the world have large sewage treatment plants to treat the millions of gallons of sewage produced every day.

Screening and settling

First, the raw sewage is passed through a screen that removes large objects, such as plastic and paper. Then the sewage passes into a large settling tank, where the solids sink to the bottom. These solids are moved to another container, where they are heated and then dried. The dried treated waste can either be burned or used as natural fertilizer on farmland.

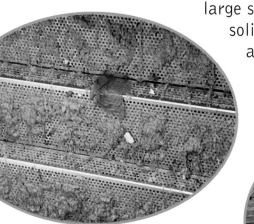

Raw sewage passes through a screen.

Sewage enters huge settling tanks.

Liquid from the settling tanks is sprinkled over gravel beds to become clean water.

Sprinkled over gravel

The liquid from the settling tank is full of nutrients and bacteria, some of which are harmful. The liquid is sprinkled over gravel beds. The liquid seeps through the beds and comes into contact with bacteria that live on the surface of the gravel. These bacteria remove all the nutrients in the water and kill harmful bacteria. Clean water drains out of the bottom of the gravel beds and is emptied into a river.

Investigate: What happens to sewage?

Some homes are connected to the sewage system and the sewage is piped away through drains. Other homes have a large tank in the ground, called a septic tank, where the sewage collects. It has to be emptied regularly. Can you find out what happens to the sewage in your home? Is it piped away or is there a septic tank? Where is your local sewage treatment plant? Many sewage treatment plants have open days when people can visit to find out more.

⬤ Canna lilies can be used to clean water. These engineers are testing the water that drains out of treatment beds in India.

Sewage ponds

Not all countries have sewage treatment plants. Some countries, such as Israel and India, pump the sewage into shallow ponds. The water in the ponds is heated by the sun, and bacteria in the water break down the sewage. Then the water pumped through a series of ponds, where it gradually becomes cleaner.

Large fish called carp are often kept in the pond. They eat the sewage and when they are large enough, they can be caught and eaten.

In Focus: Using plants to clean water

A natural way to clean water is to grow fast-growing grass that lives in shallow water, such as reeds or canna lilies. The plants are rooted in shallow beds and dirty water is circulated around their roots. Bacteria around the roots break down the sewage and the plants take up the nutrients. By the time the water drains out at the other end, it is clean enough to enter a river.

Water for farming

Farming uses huge amounts of water every day. Crops need a good supply of water if they are to grow well and produce a large yield. If there is insufficient rainfall, the plants need to be watered by a process called irrigation. In some countries up to two-thirds of the water used is used in farming.

⬥ A child fills watering cans to water his family's crops by hand.

Irrigating plants

Irrigation is common in drier parts of world, such as California, Australia, and Pakistan. Water is pumped from rivers and lakes and carried by pipe or channel to irrigate fields. The water can be sprayed on the crops or dripped on the soil around the plants. It is important to control the amount of water that is taken from rivers. If too much is taken, the water levels in the river fall and aquatic wildlife suffers.

Investigate: Hydroponics

Hydroponics is soil-less farming, where the crops are planted in tanks of nutrient-rich water rather than soil. The nutrient levels in the water are carefully controlled so that the plants get everything they require. You could try this yourself. Buy some seeds of a fast-growing salad plant, such as lettuce. Place a thick wad of cotton in the bottom of a plastic container and sprinkle a few seeds on top. Add water so that the paper is moist and leave on a sunny windowsill. Within a few days, the seeds will germinate and grow into lettuce plants. Each day, add water to the paper so the lettuce plants do not dry up. Every few days, add a few drops of a liquid plant fertilizer to the water.

Poor irrigation

Irrigation has to be carried out carefully, since poor irrigation is as bad as no irrigation. If too much water is poured over the crops, the soil becomes waterlogged, and the plant roots die. If too much water evaporates from the surface of the soil, salts are drawn from deep in the soil up to the surface. This leaves a salty crust over the soil, which very few plants can survive. This problem is called salinization and it is affecting large areas of irrigated land, especially in Australia and Pakistan.

⏷ In 1960, the Aral Sea was the world's fourth largest lake. Now it is one quarter of its original size.

In Focus: The Aral Sea

One part of the world that has suffered greatly from too much water extraction is the Aral Sea, a huge inland sea that lies between Kazakhstan and Uzbekistan. Since the 1960s, the Aral Sea has shrunk, and now it is a fraction of its original size. It may disappear completely by 2020. The Aral Sea receives most of its water from two major rivers, but most of this water has been diverted to irrigate fields of cotton crops. What little water that remains is heavily polluted from industry.

Water forever?

Water is an important natural resource. As the world's population increases, so, too, does the amount of water used each day. The activities of people are disrupting the water cycle and causing climates to change.

Trees, water, and climate

Forests hold a lot of water. When a large area of trees is cleared, the ground is left bare and unprotected. When it rains, the water runs straight off the ground into rivers. This may cause local flooding. The loss of trees means that less water is stored in the soil. Also, there is no evaporation of water from the trees' leaves into the atmosphere. The air becomes drier and there are fewer clouds. This means there is less rain. As a result, over time the climate of the area changes.

Investigate: Saving water

Some simple things that will help to save water:

- don't leave the faucet running while you are brushing your teeth;
- have a shower instead of a bath;
- if you have to run the faucet for some hot water, save the water you've used in a container and use it to water the yard;
- use the "low flush" button on the toilet or put a brick in the cistern of the toilet so that less water is flushed;
- use a water barrel to collect rainwater for watering the yard.

◀ Dams are built across many rivers to collect water that can be piped to homes.

28

● Deforestation removes the trees and leaves the soil exposed to the wind, sun, and rain.

In Focus: Recycling water

Its not just individuals that can help to save water, industry can help, too. Manufacturing industry can use less water for cleaning, cooling and washing. For example, if an aluminum rolling mill reused the water it uses for cooling, it could cut its water use by 93 percent.

Some factories may be able to reuse water, and with the installation of more efficient machinery, could reduce the amount of water they use.

The building industry can build new homes and offices that are fitted with devices to collect rain water from the roof, so it can be stored in tanks underground for use in the summer. New faucet designs can be used that limit the amount of water flowing out each time the faucet is turned on.

Climate change

The burning of coal, oil, and gas, and clearance of forests is causing the temperature of the Earth's surface to increase. This is called global warming. One of the effects of global warming is climate change. Some parts of the world may become drier and warmer and suffer a fall in rainfall. The climate of southern Spain, for example, may become more like North Africa. Other areas may become wetter and suffer from more extreme weather events, such as storms and strong winds. These changes will affect the crops that can be grown and the types of industries in a region.

● This stream is full of soil that has been washed off the land by heavy rain.

Glossary

algae Simple plants found in water, such as seaweeds, and the tiny green plants that float near the surface of water.

antifreeze A substance that lowers the freezing point of a substance so that it does not freeze so easily.

aquatic Living in water.

aquifer A layer of rock that holds water.

atmosphere The layer of air that surrounds the Earth.

atom The smallest unit of matter. A water molecule consists of two atoms of hydrogen and one of oxygen.

climate The usual pattern of weather in a place.

condensation The change in state from gas to liquid.

delta A triangular area of silt and other deposits in the mouth of a river.

detergent A soap, a cleaning agent.

diarrhea A gut problem, sometimes called "having the runs," when the body passes watery waste.

estuary The mouth of a river where fresh river water mixes with salty seawater.

evaporation The change in state from liquid to gas.

famine A situation when there is not enough food for people and they suffer from starvation.

fertilizer Nutrients that are added to the soil to make crops grow larger and faster.

freezing point The point at which a liquid turns to a solid.

glacier A slow-moving river of ice that moves downhill.

hydrological cycle The water cycle.

hydroponics Growing plants without soil.

impermeable Describing a material, such as a rock, that does not allow water to pass through.

irrigation The artificial watering of crops.

marine Relating to the sea.

meander A bend in a river.

molecule The smallest particle of a compound that contains one or more atoms.

monsoon Seasonal winds that blow in different directions at different times of year, and which bring heavy rains for part of the year.

organism A living thing.

parasite An organism that lives in or on another organism and does harm to that organism, for example, a tapeworm that lives in the gut of animals such as dogs and sheep.

pesticide A chemical that farmers use to kill pests, such as insects.

pollute To contaminate.

salinization When soil becomes too salty for plants to grow in it.

sediment Particles such as sand, silt, and clay that are carried by a river.

septic tank An underground storage tank for waste water from a home.

sewage Semiliquid waste from the bathroom and kitchen.

slurry Liquid waste that contains feces and urine from farm animals.

surface tension The attraction between water molecules at the surface of a liquid.

vapor A gas.

virus A tiny organism that can only be seen using the most powerful microscopes, and which infects other organisms and causes disease.

weather The conditions that exist at a particular time, for example, how rainy, windy, or sunny it is.

wilting When leaves become floppy and lose support due to lack of water.

Further Information

Books

Cycles in Nature: The Water Cycle
by Theresa Greenaway
(Raintree, 2000)

The Life and Times of a Drop of Water
by Angela Royston
(Raintree, 2007)

Water For All
by Sally Morgan
(Sea to Sea Publications, 2007)

Web Sites

Due to the changing nature of Internet links, PowerKids Press has developed an online list of Web sites related to the subject of this book. This site is updated regularly. Please use this link to access this list:
www.powerkidslinks.com/natc/water

Index